Where People Live

Scott White

NATIONAL GEOGRAPHIC LEARNING | **CENGAGE**

Acknowledgments

Grateful acknowledgment is given to the authors, artists, photographers, museums, publishers, and agents for permission to reprint copyrighted material. Every effort has been made to secure the appropriate permission. If any omissions have been made or if corrections are required, please contact the Publisher.

LEXILE® is a trademark of MetaMetrics, Inc., and is registered in the United States and abroad. Copyright © 2018 MetaMetrics, Inc. All rights reserved.

This book has been officially leveled by using the F&P Text Level Gradient™ System. Neither Heinemann nor Fountas and Pinnell have produced, endorsed, or sponsored this product, nor are they affiliated with the Publisher or responsible for this product.

Photographic Credits

Cover: (c) fototrav/Getty Images. **Title Page** (c) Burgess Blevins/Getty Images; **03** (r) Tom Fowlks/Shutterstock Offset; **04–05** (t) Godong/Alamy Stock Photo; **04** (l) Dennis Walton/Getty Images, (r) Olena Tur/Shutterstock.com; **05** (b) Tom Cockrem/Getty Images; **06** (c) Ashley Cooper pics/Alamy Stock Photo; **06–07** (c) AP Photo/MTI.Zsolt Szigetvary; **07** (r) Peter Adams/Getty Images; **08** (c) © Eye Ubiquitous/age fotostock; **09** (t) PHOTO 24/Getty Images, (b) Ryan McVay/Getty Images; **10** (c) National Geographic Creative/Alamy Stock Photo; **11** (l) © age fotostock/ Alamy Stock Photo, (r) Rainer Mirau/Robert Harding; **12** (l) wyndy25/Getty Images, (r) © David Gubernick/ age fotostock; **13** (c) © Nicolas Marino/age fotostock; **14** (l) Rainer Mirau/Robert Harding, (cl) Ariel Skelley/ Getty Images, (cr) © Hari Mahidhar/Dinodia Photo/age fotostock, (r) © Dinodia Photo/age fotostock; **15** (tl) Ryan McVay/Getty Images, (tc) SteveDF/Getty Images, (bl) Cedric E/Shutterstock.com, (bc) Christian Kober/Aurora Photos; **16** (c) Yann Arthus-Bertrand/Getty Images.

For product information and technology assistance, contact us at Customer & Sales Support, 888-915-3276

For permission to use material from this text or product, submit all requests online at **www.cengage.com/permissions**

Further permissions questions can be emailed to **permissionrequest@cengage.com**

National Geographic Learning | Cengage
1 Lower Ragsdale Drive
Building 1, Suite 200
Monterey, CA 93940

National Geographic Learning, a Cengage company, is a provider of quality core and supplemental educational materials for the PreK–12, adult education, and ELT markets. Cengage is a leading provider of customized learning solutions with employees residing in nearly 40 different countries and sales in more than 125 countries around the world. Find your local representative at **NGL.Cengage.com/RepFinder**.

Visit National Geographic Learning online at **NGL.Cengage.com/school**

ISBN: 978-0-3570-4846-7

Printed in the United States of America

Print Number: 02
Print Year: 2020

Contents

Think and Discuss

People live in many different places.
Talk about these different places.

a cold place

a hot place

a dry place

a wet place

Living in Hot Places

Some people live in hot places.
How do people live in these places?

People need shade in hot places.

People use fans to keep cool.

This woman's clothes help protect her from the hot sun.

Living in Cold Places

Some people live in cold places.
How do people live in these places?

These clothes help the children keep warm.

This snowplow clears a road.

This house has a fire to help people keep warm.

Living in Wet Places

Some people live in wet places.
How do people live in these places?

Some people build houses on stilts.

Sometimes people use umbrellas to stay dry.

Some people use boats as shops.

Living in Dry Places

Some people live in dry places.
How do people live in these places?

People use this water tank to catch water when it rains.

This pipe brings water from far away.

People get water from this well in the ground.

Use What You Learned

Talk about these pictures.
What do they show you about different places?

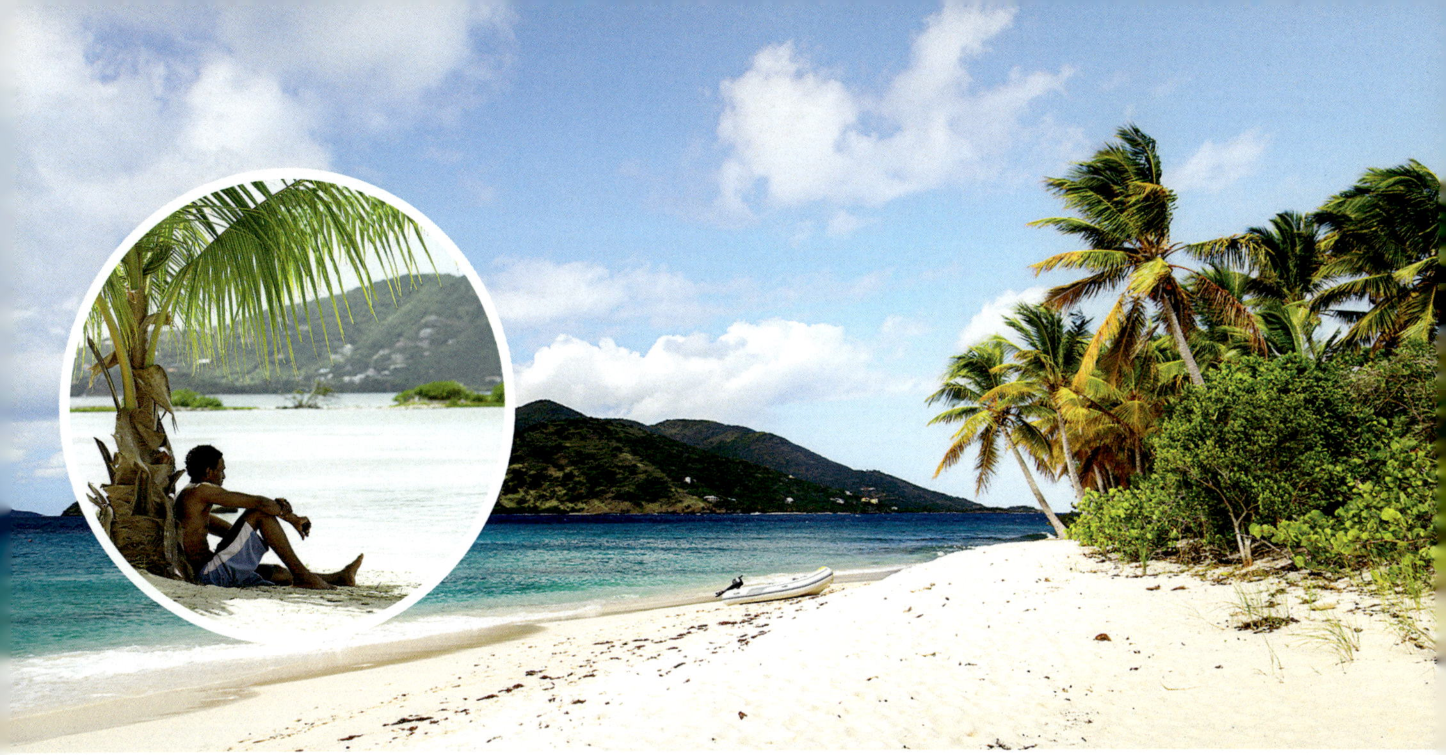

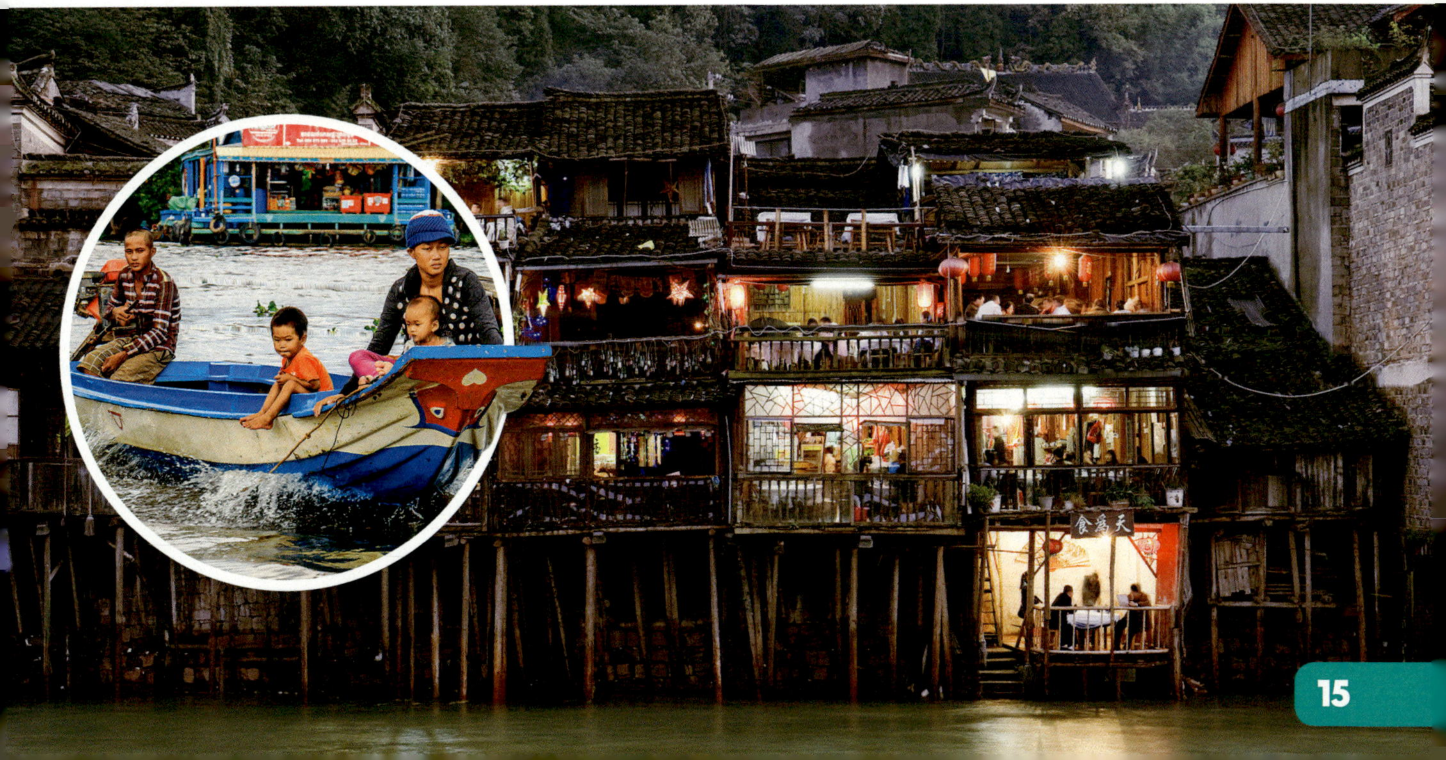

Index